BARREL

OF

CHUCKLES

Edited by
ANN McGOVERN

Illustrated by Allan Jaffee

SCHOLASTIC BOOK SERVICES
NEW YORK · TORONTO · LONDON · AUCKLAND · SYDNEY · TOKYO

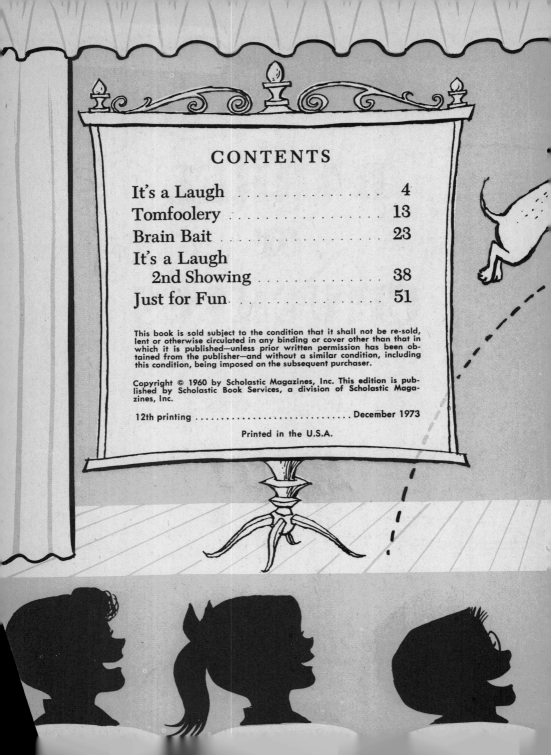

CONTENTS

Copyright © 1960 by Scholastic Magazines, Inc. This edition is published by Scholastic Book Services, a division of Scholastic Magazines, Inc.

12th printing . . . . December 1973

Printed in the U.S.A.

IT'S A LAUGH

Boys Against the Girls

HE: I'm looking for a beautiful girl.

SHE: Well, here I am.

HE: Swell, you can help me look.

SHE *(dimpling)*: Can you change a dime for me?

HE *(eagerly)*: I'd be glad to!

SHE: Then will you please change this dime into a quarter?

HE *(trying to impress her)*: My father has George Washington's watch in his collection.

SHE *(not impressed)*: Is that so? My father has Adam's apple!

HE: This music I'm playing is quite difficult.

SHE: I wish it were impossible.

HE *(at the movies)*: Can you see all right?

SHE: Yes.

HE: Can you hear all right?

SHE: Yes.

HE: Is your seat comfortable?

SHE: Yes.

HE: Would you mind changing places with me?

Boys Against the Girls

Why didn't the baseball catcher meet Cinderella?
Because he missed the ball.

SHE: If you don't stop playing that saxophone, I'll
go out of my mind.
HE: It's too late. I stopped playing an hour ago.

SHE (*at a birthday party*): That's the fourth time
you've gone back for more ice cream and cake.
Doesn't it embarrass you?
HE: Why should it? I tell the hostess it's for you!

SHE: Ouch! That water is so hot it burned my hand.
HE: Serves you right. You should have felt it before
you put your hand in it.

TED: Hi, Ed! How's your
girl friend coming along
with her diet?
ED: Just fine! She's dis-
appeared!

ROMEO: Juliet, dearest, I'm burning with love for you.

JULIET: Come now, Romeo, don't make a fuel of yourself.

SHE *(taking a picture of him)*: Look pleasant, please. As soon as I snap the picture, you can resume your normal expresssion.

SHE: I took the recipe for this cake out of the cookbook.

HE: Good, it should never have been there in the first place.

TEACHER: This is the fifth day this week you've had to stay in after school. What have you to say for yourself?

SAM: I'm very glad it's Friday.

BOY ESKIMO: What would you say if I told you I pushed my dog team a hundred miles through ice and snow just to tell you I love you?

GIRL ESKIMO: I'd say that was a lot of mush!

How Do You Like School?

Why was the United Nations concerned when a waiter dropped a platter of turkey?

It meant the fall of Turkey, the ruin of Greece, and the breaking up of China.

What did Paul Revere say at the end of his ride?
"Whoa."

What did Lewis and Clarke say before they reached the Pacific Ocean?
"Long time no sea!"

TEACHER: Jay, you're late again. What's your excuse this time?

JAY: I had to sit down in the middle of the street. A sign said, *"No Jay Walking!"*

Closed, Of Course!

TEACHER: What ten-letter word starts with gas?
BOB: Automobile.

TEACHER: Why didn't you answer me?
BILL: I did. I shook my head.
TEACHER: You didn't expect me to hear it rattle clear up here, did you?

JANE: Water attracts electricity.
TEACHER: What tests have you made to prove it?
JANE: Every time I'm in the bathtub, the phone rings.

TEACHER: Can anyone tell me what a comet is.
LULU: It's a star with a tail.
TEACHER: Can you name a comet?
LULU: Er—er—Lassie.

Animal Cracks

Two turtles decided to stop in for a soda. Just as they entered the drug store, it began to rain. The big turtle said to the little turtle, "Go home and get the umbrella."

The little turtle said, "I will, if you promise not to drink my soda."

Two years later, the big turtle said to himself, "I guess he is never coming back. I may as well drink his soda."

A voice called from outside the door, "If you touch that soda, I won't go home and get the umbrella."

DIM: Our dog is just like one of the family.

WIT: Really? Which one?

A lion who lived in the jungle met an ant. The lion growled and said to the ant, "Why aren't you big and strong like me?"

The little ant looked up at the lion and answered, "Gosh, man, I've been sick!"

ANIMAL DOCTOR: What seems to be the matter, Mrs. Kangaroo?

MRS. KANGAROO: I don't know. I haven't been feeling jumpy lately.

A fisherman was walking home when he met a friend. "Where are you going with that lobster?" his friend asked.

"I'm taking him home for dinner," the fisherman replied.

Just then the lobster spoke, "I've already had my dinner. Take me to a movie!"

A cowboy riding his horse saw a little dog running down the road.

"Hi," said the dog.

"Hi," said the cowboy.

A few minutes later, the cowboy said out loud, "That's funny. I didn't know dogs could talk."

The horse turned and looked at the cowboy.

"You learn something new every day," said the horse.

CUSTOMER (*in a pet shop*): I like this dog but his legs are too short.

CLERK: Too short? Why, madam, they reach right down to the floor.

One of King Arthur's knights ran into the inn.

"Can you lend me a horse?" the knight asked the innkeeper. "My steed is too weary to go another step."

"Sir Knight," the innkeeper said. "I have no horse. The only animal I have is that big, old dog in the corner there."

"Very well," said the knight. "I will ride him."

"Oh no, sir!" the innkeeper cried. "I wouldn't send a knight out on a dog like this!"

When does a leopard change spots?
When he moves from place to place.

TOMFOOLERY

Brags

Daffy Definitions

Silly Stunts

DOCTOR PROCTOR

Sappy Skit

13

Blow-Away

Say to a friend: "I'll place five pieces of paper on my hand. You tell me exactly how many pieces to blow away. The others will remain on my hand."

It seems an impossible task to blow away some of the pieces of paper and not to move the others. But it's easy when you know how. Simply place your *other* hand on the pieces you want to stay put. With one puff, the loose pieces will blow off. (Maybe then you'd better blow away, too!)

Give-Away

Which of your friends would turn down your offer of a quarter? (Unless he is wise to your tricks!) Tell your friend that if he can tear a square piece of paper into four equal parts you will give him a quarter.

When he has finished carefully tearing the paper, examine the pieces gravely. Pretend to measure each piece to see that there are four equal quarters. Then say: "Very good. Very good indeed." Now hand him one of the torn pieces—and get ready to run!

Twenty-five *cents?* Who said anything about *money?*

Go-Away

Say to a friend: "I'm the greatest magician of them all. Write anything you choose on any piece of paper. Now fold the paper in half. Put it on the floor and cover it with your foot. I can't see what you have written, but I'll tell you what is on your paper."

Now pretend to concentrate very hard. Don't say anything for a minute. Then say, "Ah, the answer is becoming clearer now. I see something on the paper. It is — yes — it is *your foot!*"

Hot-Foot-It-Away

Here's what you say: "I can touch a book outside and inside without opening the cover."

Here's what you do: Take the book outside the room, then bring it back into the room.

Easy Money

Here's the boast: "I can make two coins appear from one."

Here's the trick: Fill a glass half full of water. Drop a dime into the water, and put a plate on top of the glass. Carefully turn the plate and the glass upside down. Then ask your friend to look through the side of the glass. He will see two coins, and *the one on top* will look like a quarter!

Hard Counting

"Let's see how good you are at counting," you tell a friend.

"What comes after ninety-nine?"

Of course your friend will say one hundred.

"What comes after nine hundred ninety-nine?" you ask.

Your friend will say one thousand.

Now ask quickly, "What comes after nine thousand ninety-nine?"

Your friend will probably answer without thinking, "Ten thousand."

But your friend will be wrong.

The next number after 9,099 is 9,100.

It's Mighty Hard to:

Write your name on a piece of paper —

    IF the paper is stuck to your forehead with a little paste.

Stand at arm's length from your friend and move one step towards him —

    IF he places his thumb against the middle of your chest.

Put your left hand where your right hand can't reach it —

    IF you don't know this joke. The trick is to put your left hand on your right elbow.

Fold a medium piece of paper from your notebook in half eight times —

    IF — no ifs, no buts. You won't be able to do this!

Goofy Guy's

DUCK
A chicken in snowshoes.

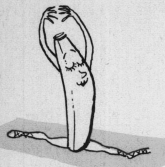

BANANA SPLIT
An acrobatic fruit.

COLD WAR
Snowball fight.

TELEPHONE BOOTH
A chatter box.

ALARM CLOCK
Something to scare the daylights into yo

Dizzy Definitions

CATERPILLAR
A worm wearing a sweater.

MISCHIEF
The chief's daughter.

BAND AID
Fund for needy musicians.

MOSQUITO
The original skin diver.

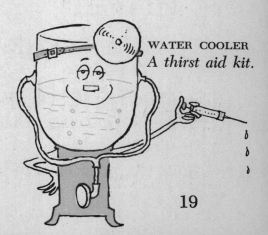

WATER COOLER
A thirst aid kit.

FIRECRACKER
A hot cookie.

19

SKIT'S EASY

Want something to do that's tricky and gay?
  It is and it isn't quite like a play.
You don't have to act and you don't have to sing,
  When you put on a skit it's the *joke* that's the thing.

For scenes and for costumes — you don't need much stuff,
  A mustache, a sign, or a hat is enough.
So gather your jokes be they whole or half-wit,
  String them together — and put on your skit!

SCENE: Doctor's Office

JOE *(running in):* Oh, doctor, I'm sorry to be so late.

DOCTOR *(frowning):* Doesn't your watch tell you the time?

JOE: Oh, no. I have to look at it.

20

DOCTOR: Now tell me, what's your trouble?

JOE *(holding his stomach)*: I'm so worried. I swallowed a roll of film.

DOCTOR: Relax. I'm sure nothing will develop. Next!

(Jane enters. Doctor examines her bandaged finger.)

JANE: Oh, doctor, tell me! Will I be able to play the piano when my finger gets better?

DOCTOR: Of course.

JANE: I never could play the piano before!

(Jane runs out happily. Enter Susie.)

DOCTOR: Well, I see you look a little thinner.

SUSIE: Yes, I've been exercising regularly. Guess what! This morning I touched the floor without bending my knees.

DOCTOR: Excellent! How did you do that?

SUSIE: I fell out of bed. By the way, my brother is the next patient.

DOCTOR: Call your brother immediately.

SUSIE: I don't think he'll come if I call him immediately.

DOCTOR: *(impatiently):* Why not?

SUSIE: His name is Sam!

(Exit Susie. Enter Sam.)

SAM *(hand over eye):* Oh doctor, what can I do for my black eye?

DOCTOR: Wow! Who gave you that shiner?

SAM: No one gave it to me. I had to fight for it.

NURSE: *(bursting in):* An emergency outside!

DOCTOR: What is it? Who's sick?

NURSE: No one's sick, exactly. The lady outside says she went riding on a gentleman horse.

DOCTOR: What on earth is a *gentleman* horse.

NURSE: She says that everytime the horse came to a fence, he let her go over first. Here she comes.

(Enter Lady.)

LADY: Oh doctor, how my leg hurts!

DOCTOR: Here's something to relieve the pain. Rub it on your leg.

LADY: Oh, oh, ouch. Next time I'll ride a horse with no manners! Will this medicine make my leg smart?

DOCTOR: *(in digust):* If it does, try rubbing some on your head!

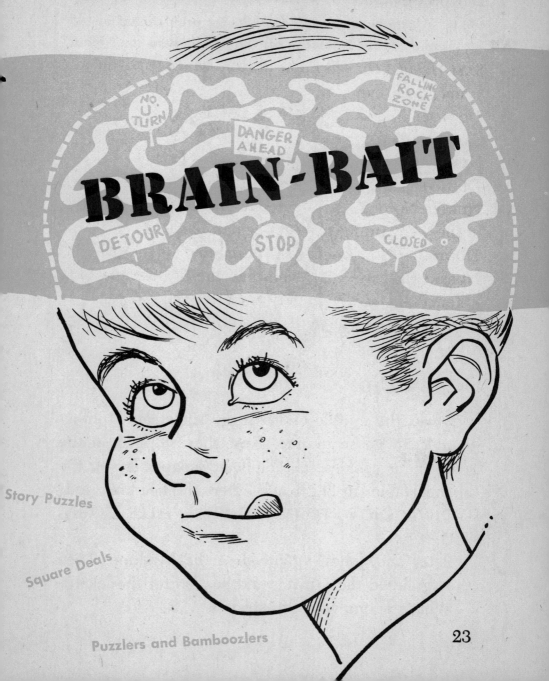

BRAIN-BAIT

Story Puzzles

Square Deals

Puzzlers and Bamboozlers

Dippy Dip

It was the middle of February. Peter and Johnny wanted to go swimming. First they stopped in the kitchen for cookies. The daily newspaper lay on the kitchen table. In big, black letters the headline said: WORST SNOWSTORM OF YEAR HITS COUNTRY.

Peter and Johnny glanced at the headline. Then they grabbed their towels and headed for the lake.

What's wrong with this story?

24

Night-Mare

A trainer once owned a very valuable race horse which he decided to enter in the Kentucky Derby. A few days before the race, he kept the horse in a stable which was only a block away from the railroad tracks. Since he had no assistant, he hired an old man as night watchman to look after the horse.

On the morning of the day before the race, the trainer went to the stable to see his horse. There he found the night watchman in a very excited state.

"Please don't enter your horse in the race," the old man begged. "I had a nightmare last night — a dream of evil omen. I dreamed the horse broke out of this stable and ran down the railroad tracks. An express train struck the horse and killed him."

The trainer immediately fired the old man. Why?

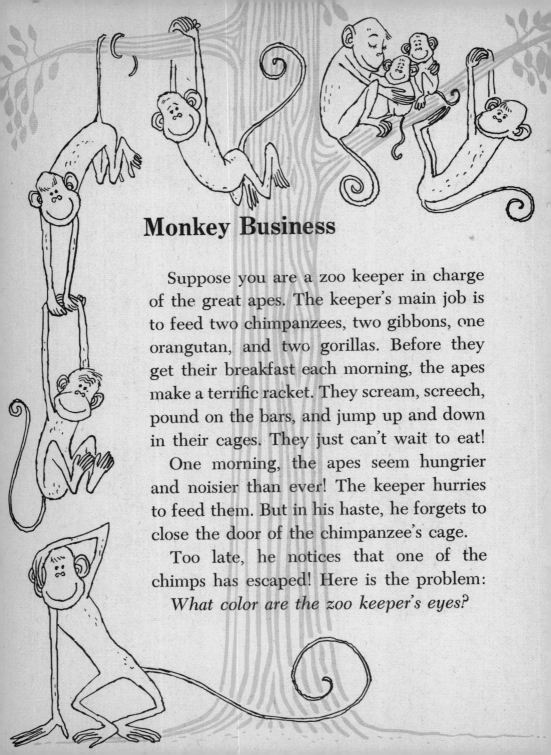

Monkey Business

Suppose you are a zoo keeper in charge of the great apes. The keeper's main job is to feed two chimpanzees, two gibbons, one orangutan, and two gorillas. Before they get their breakfast each morning, the apes make a terrific racket. They scream, screech, pound on the bars, and jump up and down in their cages. They just can't wait to eat!

One morning, the apes seem hungrier and noisier than ever! The keeper hurries to feed them. But in his haste, he forgets to close the door of the chimpanzee's cage.

Too late, he notices that one of the chimps has escaped! Here is the problem: *What color are the zoo keeper's eyes?*

Gurgle Gurgle

Just for the fun of it, imagine you are about to take a bath in a soundproof bathroom. There are no windows. There is only one door, and it locks automatically from the outside when shut. You shut the door, and turn on the water in the bathtub. Suddenly you discover that something has gone wrong with the faucets. You can't turn off the water! What to do? If you call for help no one will hear you because of the soundproof walls. You can't get out because the door is locked from the outside.

How can you keep from drowning?

GOOFY: "Grab a lifesaver?"

Square Deals

Each of these puzzles contains three words which read the same from top to bottom as they read across. Clues are given for each word. Fill in the empty spaces with the correct letters, and you'll have a square deal!

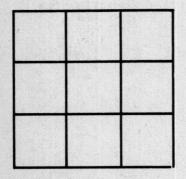

1. Flying animal.
   What you breathe.
   Attempt.

2. Make use of.
   Cunning.
   What you see with.

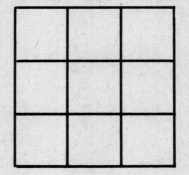

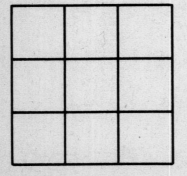

3. Be in debt.
   False Hair.
   Good for breakfast.

4. Drink made from leaves.
Finish.
Total up numbers.

5. Fuel for cars.
Noah's boat.
Where clouds are.

6. Two peas in a ___ ___ ___ .
You row with this.
Opposite of wet.

It's a Mystery

Tom, Jack, and Michael are traveling on a school bus with their teacher. Suddenly the bus enters a long and dusty tunnel.

At the other end of the tunnel, the teacher notices that all three boys' foreheads have been smudged with dirt. She decides to find out which boy is the smartest.

She tells the boys: "Each of you look at the other two. If you see someone whose forehead is smudged with dirt, raise your hand." All three raise their hands.

"Now," she goes on, "as soon as you know for certain if you are smudged or not, put down your hand." All three keep their hands raised for a few minutes. Then, with a smile, Jack puts down his hand.

"I know that my forehead is smudged," he announces.

How does he know?

Private Eye

Private-Eye Pete, the great detective, is on a big case. He's been on the trail of a desperado for months. And now, great news: In this morning's mail, there's a letter from his assistant, telling where the outlaw's hideout is. Eagerly, Pete tears open the envelope. Alack and alas! The letter is in semi-code and Private-Eye Pete does not know the key to the code.

Here's the letter:

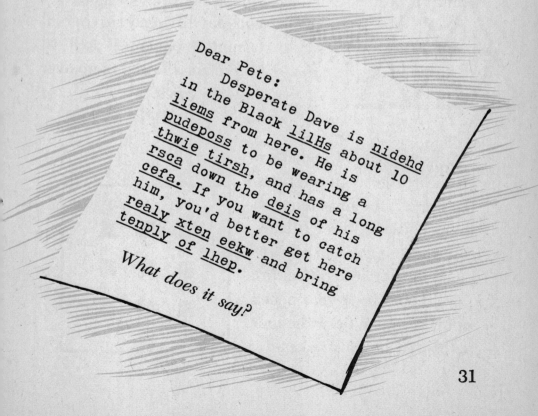

Dear Pete:
Desperate Dave is nidehd in the Black lilHs about 10 liems from here. He is pudeposs to be wearing a thwie tirsh, and has a long rsca down the deis of his cefa. If you want to catch him, you'd better get here realy xten eekw and bring tenply of lhep.

What does it say?

Figure It Out

What is this drawing? Just a design? No, it's the secret hiding place for fifteen different letters. Can you find them all? One, two, fifteen —GO!

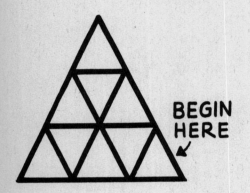

BEGIN HERE

Can you trace this diagram without lifting your pencil from the paper? Watch it! You're not allowed to go over any line twice.

Bill will have a busy day. He has to go to four stores, the library, the museum, and to the houses of three friends. Bill wants to go from place to place in four straight routes.

Without lifting your pencil from the paper, draw the four paths that he must take.

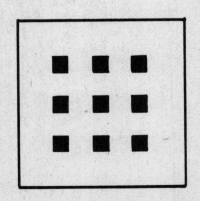

32

Goofy's FUNWORDS

Print these words ACROSS:

1. What have tongues yet never talk?
4. What did the hat say to the hatrack? "You stay here while I go on _ _ _ _ _."
5. What is the difference between an organist and a cold in the head? One knows the _ _ _ _ _ and the the other stops the nose.

Print these words DOWN:

1. Shooting _ _ _ _ _ should be made to observe the game laws. *(heavenly bodies)*
2. What state serves as a source of metal? *(Abbrev.)*
3. Why does a cat look first to one side and then to the other when it enters a room? Because it can't see both _ _ _ _ _ at once.

Goofy's FUNWORDS

Print these words ACROSS:

1. A waiter is a man who believes money grows on _ _ _ _ _.
   (rhymes with days)
4. What most resembles half a cheese?
   The _ _ _ _ _ half.
5. What is the best way to keep skunks from smelling? Cut off their
   _ _ _ _ _.

Print these words DOWN:

1. When do elephants have eight feet? When there are _ _ _ of them.
2. When butter is worth twenty cents a pound, what will a ton of coal come to?
3. Society of Intelligent Rowboats. *(Abbrev.)*

34

Whiz of a Wizard

Hand a friend a penny and a nickel. Ask your friend to hold the penny in one hand and the nickel in the other.

"I can tell in which hand you are holding the nickel," you say. "Multiply the coin in your left hand by 16. When you have the answer, nod your head."

You don't have to be a math whiz to figure this out. It is easy to multiply 16 by 1. So if your friend nods his head right away, you know he has multiplied 16 by 1. Then the coin in his left hand is a penny.

But if your friend takes a little while to do his figuring, you know he is multiplying 16 by 5. Then the coin in his left hand is a nickel.

A Special Fortuneteller

Here's the boast: Don't tell *me*. I can tell you how many people there are in your family.

Here's the trick: Ask your friend to multiply the number of brothers he has by 2. Tell him to add 3, and to multiply the sum by 5. Now ask him to add the number of his sisters and to multiply the total number by 10. Then he must add the number of other people in his family.

Now ask your friend to write down his answer. You now subtract 150 from this answer. Look carefully at the result. The first number on the left will be the number of brothers your friend has. The middle number will be the number of sisters he has. And the number on the right will tell you how many others there are in his family.

The trick always works.

For example, Jack has one brother and two sisters in his family as well as his mother and father. Here's the arithmetic you would use:

One brother x 2 = 2
Add 3 (3 plus 2) = 5
Now multiply by 5 (5 x 5) = 25
Add the number of sisters   25 plus 2 = 27
Multiply the total by 10   27 x 10 = 270
Now add the number of other people in the family
    270 plus 2 = 272
Subtract 150 from the answer

$$\begin{array}{r} 272 \\ -150 \\ \hline 122 \end{array}$$

It works!

IT'S A LAUGH
2ND
SHOWING

The Adventures of Goofy Guy

One day Goofy Guy met two old friends and invited them to his home for dinner. Goofy Guy lived on the twentieth floor of an apartment house. When they reached the house, they discovered that the elevator was out of order and that they would have to walk up the stairs.

Goofy Guy said to his friends: "The climb won't seem so hard if we pass the time away. One of you should sing, the other should tell a joke, and I will tell a sad, sad story."

When they reached the nineteenth floor, it was Goofy's turn to tell his sad story.

He did.

"I left the key downstairs," he said.

❖   ❖   ❖

Goofy Guy was taking a train trip across the country.

At the water fountain at the end of the car, he met another passenger. They began to talk.

"I always get sick when I ride backwards on a train," Goofy Guy said.

"Why don't you ask the passenger riding opposite you to trade places?" the man suggested.

"Oh," said Goofy Guy. "I thought of that, but there wasn't anyone there."

Have you EVER seen…?

a clam bake

a pen point

a jelly roll

an ice skate

a bull doze

a cereal bowl

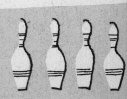

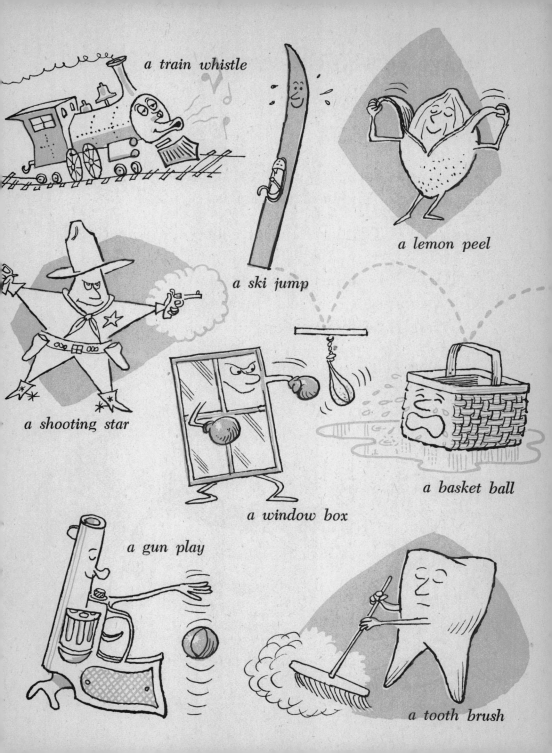

a train whistle

a ski jump

a lemon peel

a shooting star

a window box

a basket ball

a gun play

a tooth brush

Buffered Muttin

WAITER: I have boiled tongue, fried liver, and pigs' feet.

CUSTOMER: Don't tell me your troubles. Just give me a cheese sandwich and a glass of milk.

CUSTOMER: I'd like a cup of coffee and a muttered buffin.

WAITER: You mean a buffered muttin.

CUSTOMER: No, I mean a muttered buffin.

WAITER: How about making it a doughnut and milk?

CUSTOMER: I'd like some ginger ale, please.

WAITER: Pale?

CUSTOMER: No, a glass will do.

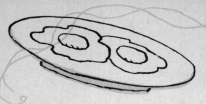

More Restaurant Jokes

DINER: Waiter, there's something the matter with the eggs you just served me.

WAITER: That's not my responsibility, sir. I only laid the table.

WAITER: Do you want your eggs turned over?

CUSTOMER: Yes! To the Museum of Natural History!

1ST CUSTOMER: What a restaurant! I ordered a fresh egg and got the freshest egg in the world: I ordered hot coffee and got the hottest coffee in the world.

2ND CUSTOMER: Yes, I know. I ordered a small steak.

DINER: Waiter, please take this steak back. I've sawed it and jabbed it and I still can't cut it.

WAITER: Sorry sir, I *can't* take it back. You've bent it.

43

Sign on a drinking fountain:

Old Faceful

Sign in a clothing shop during Christmas week:

Many Happy Returns—We Expect Them

Sign on an automobile repair shop:

WE'RE ALWAYS ON OUR TOWS

Sign advertising dachshund puppies:

GET A LONG LITTLE DOGGIE

Sign on a soft-drink counter:

PINK LEMONADE — ALL COLORS

Sign in a florist's shop:

DIRT CHEAP

Goofy Guy's Silly Signs

The Home Front

BOY: Mom, how much am I worth to you?
MOM: A million dollars.
BOY: Then could you advance me a quarter?

PAT: Pop, what should I wear with my purple and green socks?
POP: Hip boots!

SALESMAN: I'd like to see your mother, son.
BOY: She's out.
SALESMAN: Well, then, I'd like to see your dad.
BOY: He's out.
SALESMAN: Then may I come in and wait by the fire?
BOY: The fire's out, too.

MARY: I wish I had the money to buy an elephant.
MOM: What would you do with an elephant?
MARY: Who wants the elephant? I just want the money.

SUE: Pop, there was a man to see you today.
POP: Did he have a bill?
SUE: No, Pop, an ordinary nose like yours.

The Great Outdoors

A hunter hired a guide to lead him through the wilderness. The hunter soon discovered they were walking around in circles.

"We're lost," the hunter complained to the guide. "I thought you said you were the best guide in the state of Maine!"

"I am," said the guide. "But I think we are in Canada now!"

CITY BOY: Oh, what a funny-looking cow. But why hasn't it any horns?

COUNTRY BOY: There are many reasons why a cow does not have horns. Some grow horns late in life. Others are dehorned. Some breeds are not supposed to have horns. This cow does not have horns because it is a horse.

JOE: Once, hunting in Africa, I was so close to a lion I could feel his breath down my neck.

JOHNNY: What did you do?

JOE: I put my collar up.

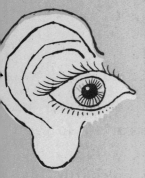

There was a young man who said, "Why
Can't I look in my ear with my eye?
If I put my mind to it
I'm sure I can do it,
You never can tell till you try!"

Susanna, a sweet little miss,
Declared roller skating was bliss.
But she knew not her fate
For a wheel off her skate
Made her end up something like this!

GOOFY'S Limerick

One day I went out to the zoo
For I wanted to see the old Gnu.
But the old Gnu was dead,
And the new Gnu, they said,
Surely knew as a Gnu he was NEW!

BAG and BAGGAGE

Why is the prairie so flat? Because the sun sets on it every night.

BOB: Are you going to take the car out in this weather?

BILL: Yes, of course. It's a driving rain, isn't it?

WILLY: Did anyone laugh when you fell on the ice?

BILLY: No, but the ice made some awful cracks.

LADY: Are you satisfied to spend your life walking the country and begging?

HOBO: No, indeed, lady. Many's the time I wished I had a car.

A man struck oil, and with his new riches built a huge mansion with three swimming pools. He filled one pool with cool water, the second pool with warm water, and the third pool he kept empty.

"Why is there no water in the third pool?" a friend asked.

"A lot of my friends can't swim," the millionaire explained.

Why is a cookbook exciting?
It has many stirring events.

Why is the letter B like a fire?
Because it makes oil boil?

What most resembles the half of an apple?
The other half.

Ten-year-old Johnny applied for a job as a grocery boy. The grocer wanted a serious-minded boy for the job. So he put Johnny to a little test.

"Well, my boy," the grocer said. "What would you do with a million dollars?"

"Oh, sir!" Johnny answered, "I wasn't expecting so much at the start."

PAULINE: What a beautiful painting! I wish I could take those lovely colors home with me.

PAINTER: You can! You're sitting on my paint box.

49

Goofy Guy's Silly Sentences

The teacher asked Goofy Guy to use the word *income* in a sentence.

Goofy Guy said, "I opened the door and in come a cat."

The teacher sighed. "No, Goofy! Try again. Use *ransom* in a sentence."

"I saw a skunk in the woods," said Goofy, "and I ran some distance away."

The teacher moaned. "Do you know what the word *handsome* means?" she asked.

"Of course I know," said Goofy. "Please hand some candy to me right away."

The teacher groaned. "Give me the word *infantry* in a sentence," she said.

Goofy thought and thought. His face lit up. "I know," Goofy said. "The infant tree grew into a tall oak."

"No, no, no!" cried the teacher. "I'll try one more time. Use the word *gruesome* in a sentence."

"Since last year," Goofy said, "I grew some."

GOOFY: "P.S. That's my teacher!"

Take a Partner

For this stunt, you need one friend, one short piece of rope, and two pieces of paper. Decide where you will stand for your tug of war. You must each put a piece of paper behind you on the floor. Now — each of you take hold of your end of the rope and pull. The trick is to pick up the paper behind you while you are pulling on the rope. The first one to do it wins, of course.

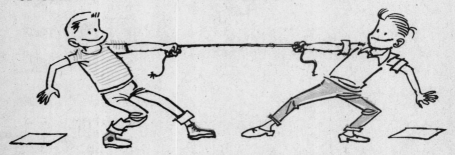

Your friend holds a short stick or pencil lightly by its end. You stand facing him. Your hand should be outstretched — even with his stick. Your friend suddenly lets go of the stick. Is your hand quicker than your eye? You must catch the stick before it falls to the floor. Sounds easy, doesn't it?

It's not!

Stop, Thief!

Put a penny on the table and leave the room. While you are gone, someone takes the coin.

Your job: To spot the criminal!

This looks like the perfect crime. But ah! No one suspects you have a partner helping you. You come back into the room. You look around accusingly. Then you ask everyone to touch your forehead. When they have all had their turn, you close your eyes, put your hand on your forehead and pretend to think deeply.

Then, with a cry of triumph, you point to the person who took the penny.

How do you know? Your partner has told you. But how? While the game was going on, you and he did not speak. Your partner waited until the guilty one touched your forehead. Then he immediately took his turn at touching you. That was the giveaway. The person who touched your forehead just before your partner did, is the one who stole the penny.

Two for Magic!

For this foolery, two heads are better than one. You must work with a secret partner. You announce to everyone: "While I am out of the room, hide any coin under a cup. By the magic of my powers, I will be able to tell you which coin is hidden."

Then you leave the room. Everyone who wants to is given a chance to check on the coin. Your partner takes this opportunity to set the handle of the cup as he would set a clock. He uses this clock code you two have agreed upon:

Handle at 12 o'clock — penny

Handle at 2 o'clock — nickel

Handle at 4 o'clock — dime

Handle at 6 o'clock — quarter

Handle at 8 o'clock — half dollar

When you come back into the room, the first thing you do is look at the position of the cup handle. Then with a deep bow, you tell your mystified audience which coin is under the cup.

Ghostly Magic

Say: "I feel the spirits are very close to us today. If you are with us, spirits, prove it by emptying a glass of water."

Do this: Fill a glass of water and cover it with paper strips so no one could possibly drink from it. Leave just enough space in the center for a straw to slip through. Tape the paper strips securely around the glass. Then turn out the lights and say: "Spirits, are you here?" When the lights come on again, the glass is empty and your friends are baffled.

Here's how: Hide a straw in your inside coat pocket. When the room is dark, insert the straw through the paper strips, drink the water, and then drop the straw back into your pocket.

Take a Card

All you need for this magic is a deck of cards and a tricky smile.

Before you amaze your friends, do this: Divide the deck into two piles. Put all the odd-numbered cards in one pile and all the even-numbered cards in the other. One pile will consist of aces, threes, sevens, nines, jacks, and kings. The other pile will consist of twos, fours, sixes, eights, tens, and queens.

Then: Say to a friend, "Pick any card from either pile." If he chooses an even-numbered card, slip it casually into the odd-numbered pile. If he chooses an odd-numbered card, be sure to slip it into the even-numbered pile.

Now ask your friend to shuffle this half deck of cards. When he hands the cards back to you, you can instantly spot the card he chose. It will be the only odd or even card in the pile.

Pop!

This trick can be carried around in your pocket. Your friend will be amazed when he opens the book of matches you hand him. Out will pop a jumping jack!

To make this popping pocket jumping jack, you need: an empty match-book, a strip of some heavy paper like typewriter paper which is 7 and ¾ inches long and ¾ of an inch wide, and a goofy-looking paper face which you can draw or cut from a magazine.

First fold the strip of paper into half-inch pleats as shown in picture A. Next, glue the funny face to one end of the strip as shown in picture B. Then, glue the other end of the strip to the inside of the match-book cover as shown in picture C. Close the cover of the match-book and try it. Ooops!

P.S. When the jack stops jumping, you need a new paper strip.

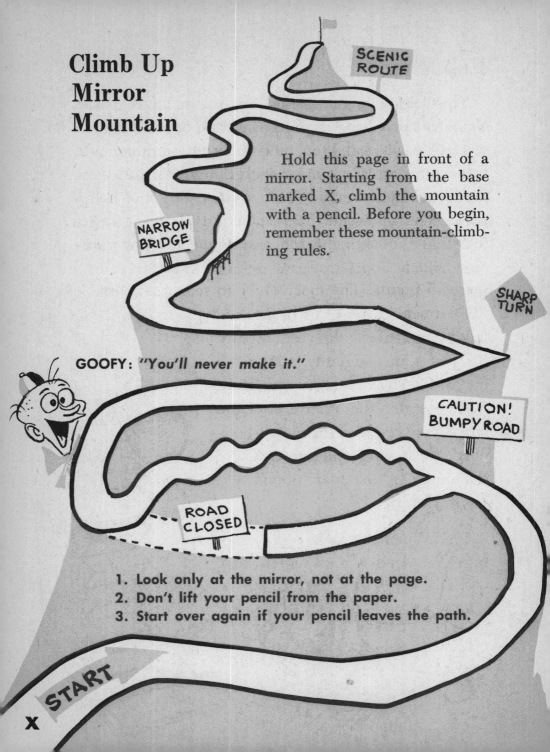

Roll 'Em

For this game, you need a large tin can, some kind of weight to keep it from rolling, and a small ball. If you play outdoors, you must play on level ground. Put the can on the ground with the weight inside (a small rock will work).

Each player stands 15 feet from the can and tries to roll the small ball into the open end. He gets three chances. Each time he rolls the ball into the can he scores 5 points. The first player to score 25 points is the winner.

Hook 'Em

You don't always need bait or the deep blue sea to go fishing. Here's a fish-at-home game. You need a cardboard box or a box cover 8 inches square. A cake box is just right. Cut 12 slits two inches long and two inches apart as shown in picture A. Now trace the fish on this page as shown in picture B or cut out your own, making it 3½ inches long and 2½ inches wide. You need 12 fish. If you paste the fish on cardboard they will be easier to play with. Number each fish on the tail from 1 to 12. Stick a paper clip on the head of each fish.

For your fishing pole, you need a pencil, a string, and another paper clip. Be sure your string is 8 inches long. Bend the paper clip into a hook as shown in picture C.

Now slip one fish into each slit, with the clip on top.

The game is to hook as many fish as you can. This game can be played with any number of players or with teams. Take turns fishing. Then you add up the numbers on the tails of the fish you catch. The players or the team with the highest score wins.

ANSWERS

page 24 — *Dippy Dip*

Fooled you! There is absolutely nothing wrong with the story. Peter and Johnny live in Florida where the weather is fine for swimming all year long.

page 25 — *Night-Mare*

The watchman had to be asleep to dream, and he should not have been asleep on the job.

page 26 — *Monkey Business*

The color of your eyes, of course. The first sentence reads: Suppose *you* are a zoo keeper in charge of the great apes.

page 27 — *Gurgle Gurgle*

Pull out the stopper or the drain.

pages 28-29 — *Square Deals*

1.

B	A	T
A	I	R
T	R	Y

2.

U	S	E
S	L	Y
E	Y	E

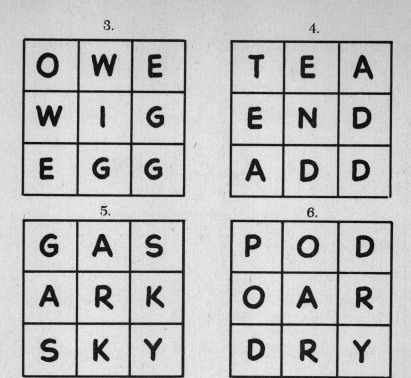

3.

O	W	E
W	I	G
E	G	G

4.

T	E	A
E	N	D
A	D	D

5.

G	A	S
A	R	K
S	K	Y

6.

P	O	D
O	A	R
D	R	Y

page 30 — *It's A Mystery*

Jack thinks: "All three of us have our hands up. I know that Tom and Michael are both smudged because I can see them. Either I am smudged or I am not smudged. Suppose I am not smudged. Then Tom would know that Michael's hand is up because Michael sees Tom's smudge. And Michael would know that Tom's hand is up because Tom sees Michael's smudge. Both Tom and Michael could easily tell that each of them is smudged. Each would drop his hand. However their hands are up. They're uncertain. Therefore, I must be smudged, too."

page 31 — *Private Eye*

Desperate Dave is hidden in the Black Hills about ten miles from here. He is supposed to be wearing a white shirt, and has a long scar down the side of his face. If you want to catch him, you'd better get here early next week and bring plenty of help.

page 32 — *Figure It Out*

E, F, H, I, K, L, M, N, P, T, V, W, X, Y, Z,

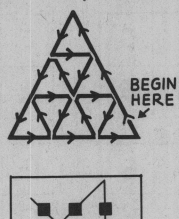

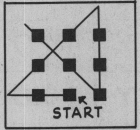

page 33 — *Funwords*

¹S	H	²O	E	³S
T	■	R	■	I
⁴A	H	E	A	D
R	■	■	■	E
⁵S	T	O	P	S

page 34 — *Funwords*

¹T	R	²A	Y	³S
W	■	S	■	I
⁴O	T	H	E	R
■	■	E	■	■
⁵N	O	S	E	S